Répondez s'il vous plaît

Sophie Smith

BookLeaf Publishing

India | USA | UK

Presentation by *BookLeaf Publishing*

Web: www.bookleafpub.com

E-mail: info@bookleafpub.com

ISBN: 9789358314403

First edition 2024

DEDICATION

I dedicate this book to anyone who is part of the 1 in 4, and has been through abuse, rape or sexual assault. I hope this helps you feel seen, heard and understood.

ACKNOWLEDGEMENT

I want to acknowledge the charities and organisations that helped me accept my diagnosis of PTSD, which include: Rape and Sexual Violence Project Birmingham (RSVP, Black Country Women's Aid (BCWA), and NHS Talking Therapies. To the therapists that helped me towards the light at the end of the tunnel, and to become a psychotherapist myself... Tracie, Lillian, Jo, Dianne, and Tom.

PREFACE

Most writers say that their inspiration starts from dreams or visions, but mine began by a nightmare I had. I was wrapped in a big yellow and black striped evidence bag, and was told by the police in this nightmare I couldn't take it off, I had to walk around until the trial with this big plastic wrap around me, clearly painting me as a victim. No one was allowed to address me by my first name, only "Exhibit A". I was unable to talk to anyone about what happened, or I would contaminate the evidence.

This nightmare was a metaphor for my life from 2019-2023.

Répondez s'il vous plaît

If only I could have taken back the invitation I
had neatly hand-written you to "RSVP" into my
life.
You returned the invitation almost completely
blank.
except for tiny specks of black ink outside the
two boxes.
I spent hours picking apart the invitation,
trying to decipher which speck was closer to
"YES" and "NO"
trying to give myself an answer for the question
you had left unanswered.

The next thing I know, you politely knock at the
door.
I race to answer, putting all things aside.
I wanted to fall with unquestionable faith into
your closed arms.
I wanted you to catch my full weight.
Instead, you pushed me aside and invited
yourself in.
"Can you take your shoes off?", I asked,
not wanting to ruin the carpet I had tried so hard
to keep clean.
You answered with an absent stare.

It was like watching a movie from above in
black and white.
the colour had faded,
losing its identity.

If only I had realized sooner
that I had superficially "fallen in love" with this
being sitting beside me,
like a child who had never seen a toy before;
who would never know there were better ones
out there.
 You were the one I had desperately craved to be
around,
and one that I would grow to fear.

I was so fixated by our newfound intimacy, that
when you turned away, I knew without even
looking down that the carpet was destroyed.
I knew I would have to dig up the floor, and I
couldn't do it alone.

"I thought you wanted me to come?", You said,
waving the invitation above my head.
"Yes, but on my own terms", I replied.

Wildflowers

3

These wildflowers, they stem from survival.
Which is engrained in every petal.
Growing away from dead roots, towards the sun
they climb -
Fighting the never-ending battle against gravity.
They weren't even planted on purpose,
they weren't chosen from seed.
Minimal nurture -
no one to water them when there's drought.
But through neglect,
it doesn't make them less beautiful.

Same Direction

Every so often I see a glimpse of my own
reflection,
and it's like running into an old friend on the
train.
Both heading in the same direction,
completely crossed by chance.

I raise a hand and wave across the carriage,
 but she looks right through me
like I'm some sort of complete stranger.
Back to my seat I retreat in silence.

"Exhibit B"

"Why won't you wear me anymore?", cried the
Pink Blouse,
alone, segregated from the rest of my clothes,
still trapped untouched inside the plastic bag
marked "Exhibit B".
"Tomorrow", I promised,
as I closed the wardrobe and chose a familiar
oversized black jumper,
instead of the blouse I had once loved.
tainted by ancient struggle and strife.
I placed the jumper over my head and yanked it
down,
concealing the cold, malnourished frame I had
grown to resent.
Standing in the mirror's opinionated glare,
I inspect and pick over the skin and bones
marked as "Exhibit C",

making sure everything was exactly how I left it.

Patchwork Skin

6

I didn't walk away from him.
I dragged every muscle
and every bone in my body
across the gravel pavement of his street,
And when I finally stitched my patchwork skin
back together,
I ran and never looked back.

Medicine

The best medicine I have received
was not mass produced by pharmaceutical
companies
making millions from people's unfortunate
ill-health.
But instead from your personalised love,
unique as DNA, and handcrafted just for me.
With the forehead kisses that killed the cancer of
memories,
the hugs that strengthened my bones,
and the touch of your lips like CPR
that gave me air in my lungs,
to breathe on my own again.

Haircut

She ran her hands through the lengths of my
golden straw.
Surely, I should feel glad that the hair he
touched will be detached from my body, and fall
to the floor.
Swept up and discarded,
buried in the ground.
The stubborn dust of months of trauma
silenced without a sound.
I cannot bear the touch of another on my hair,
it brings me back to the same old nightmare.
I sit in the chair, silently being judged by a
woman who simply doesn't know.
Who just wonders "why is she missing hair?"
"have you been tying your hair in elastic
bands?" she says
"I could feed your hair to my horses, it's like
hay!"
She tuts as she canvases my hair, tutting at the
sight and the state.
"How could you put off getting your 6-week
trim so late?"
I slump in the chair, feeling victimised again
by this woman I had once called a friend.

Quiet Mind

9

"So, what's next?" I asked my therapist.
She smiled as she said,
"To learn to have a quiet mind".
I never estimated how hard it would be
to have a mind that could hear its intuition
over the fear that trauma had left me with.

Trigger

Your words were the trigger
that fired the bullet
which ripped a hole in my deep flesh
which would never heal.

I keep the wound covered at all times
       to make myself appear strong to my
enemies,
          and even my friends.

But sometimes it bleeds through.
But no one rushes to help,
because only I can see the blood.

The First and the Last

Was I your first one?
Thinking how you were so organised,
You made me feel loved,
you knew what to say,
and exactly what to do.
I suppose I will never know now.

But I hope to be your last one.
So no one can feel the way I do.
And I've done everything I can to make sure of
that.
But I suppose that's not in my hands,
it's in yours,
and the twelve strangers on the jury.

You probably thought this was going to be a love
note…

it's not.

Hush

12

No.
I will not be hushed about things that you want
me to be silent about.
I will awake the world at 4:56am,
whispering my truth
I need not shout
The truth needn't be told in one sound wave,
But ripples that break the longstanding silence
And cause earthquakes felt by all humanity.

Swimsuit

I used to sit in the shower with a swimsuit on,
because I was too afraid to look at my body.
Imprinted with your touch
With scars that wouldn't budge
like braille telling my story.

I have claimed my body, it is all mine,
without an ounce of selfishness.
I'm learning to love every inch
Walk through fire and not flinch
And sacrifice myself with pure selflessness

Trial

As I sat behind screens in the Witness Box of
my trial
for justice and closure,
I thought it would be liberating.
But it felt like I was setting myself on fire,
For the whole world to watch me burn.
Hoping a spark would set him alight too,
And incinerate the lies to reveal the truth.

One Blood

15

I am their daughter.
In their flesh, in their tears
In the sleepless nights and unseen days,
Trying to avoid my thoughts and deepest fears.

I am their sister.
In their laughter, in their cries
Trying to avoid the hurt in the truth,
By hiding it in white lies.

But we are one blood together,
A collective being.
So when you attacked me,
You attacked them too.

Fugitive

For too long I have fled from emotional cold
wars,
finding temporary solace in the hands of another
abuser,
who would slowly take the bricks from the
shelter,
to throw them at me.
And the rain would pour down on me
through gaps in the roof.

For too long I have been someone else's fugitive
because I thought the shelter of my own body
was not enough.
But one day I will find refuge in my own body,
and feel safe in it too.

ID

Approaching the gate,
I stop.
Frantically searching for a 3-year-old university
identification card.
I play tug of war in my pocket,
and at last, it is freed from the grip of some
cheap earphones.

The long navy-blue lanyard escapes from my
hand as it falls to the floor.
I stop.
And I look at it there for a second.

Surely that's not mine?
 It looks nothing like me.

People rush by, swiping their cards and moving
on.
I reach down slowly, my books heavy in my
arms, swaying my balance.
I pick up the ID card, scratched, faded and worn
down from wear and tear.

But the girl with long blonde hair is still there

On Paper

For many, they will only know me through a
piece of paper.
My life's trauma stripped bare,
my case files sat on a desk.

Please spare a moment
      for my grieving -

For my trauma cannot be closed like a book,
when the chapter has not ended yet.

Better Weather

Today I'm spending the day in bed,
     wishing for better weather.
Inside my own personal thunderstorm,
isolating myself for safe measure.

When the rain comes down,
     it doesn't trickle - it floods.
But forecasts are useless
and often misjudged.

So, I wait and pray,
to one day bask in the sun,
and feel the light filtering into my pale skin.

No Applause

Today, as normal
I am fighting a war.
Even if I win the battle,
there will be no applause.

An audience looks on
with judgemental eyes,
For I have no armour,
because this battle came on as a surprise.

All the same,
I put on my war paint -
which is simply a smile,
that I call a brave face.

PERPETRATOR

Downstairs on your sofa I slept so soundly,
Heavily intoxicated to glaze over the broken
pane of reality,
I was so blissfully unaware of what was
happening around me.

I will never understand the thoughts that went
through your head,
What drives a person to do what you did?
Why you didn't leave me to sleep, and go
upstairs to bed?

I'm living in one of the stories you hear every
day on the news, the ones that everyone's shared
on Facebook, quickly skimmed over and read,
But life is like a lottery, and the odds were so
slim,
I thought it would happen to someone else
instead.

When I thought of rape and assault, I imagined it
would be a random attack,
Walking alone at night, streetlights illuminating
women as targets.

I told myself if it happened, I'd kick, I'd scream,
I'd bite and fight back.

Now you're forcing yourself onto me, and
ripping out my long blonde hair,
I try to let out a scream or even a small sound,
But my lungs just don't have the air.

I remember sitting in the police station,
recounting what happened to an officer I didn't
know well.
I sit rigidly upright, frozen solid in the middle of
summer,
I was going through my own personal kind of
hell.

Now I've blocked you on all forms of social
media, ended my placement and cut all ties
All that I have left is questions:
Why me, and why lie?

I've had so many sleepless nights since, thinking
"Where did it all go wrong?"
You talked to me so sweetly, you listened to me
tentatively,
Was using me for your own pleasure really your
intention all along?

I used to see the good in people, but now I see
nothing at all.
For you, the warning bells cried out,
But I didn't hear their call.

With the physical cuts and bruises, they healed
and eventually faded away.
But with the countless labels of mental illness
handed to me, as a "gift" from you,

I relive the trauma every single night and day.

The memories, they haunt me, deep in my mind
they like to lurk.
They're with me everywhere I go, sending me
constant reminders.
They follow me like a dark cloud over my head
to work.

It's always at night time that I begin to overthink
and fret,
How could this have happened?
Surely it didn't.
How did a seemingly-normal man like you,
could slip so easily through the net?

I look at girls close to me, my friends, my
cousins, and my sisters.

And now I fear for when they leave for school in
the morning,
Because a perpetrator could be their teacher.

I have so many questions with no answers to,
that I will most likely never know.
I'm trying to make peace with it,
But why did this happen? I clearly told you no.

I used to admire your confidence, something I
didn't have for my own.
But that confidence turned out to be arrogance,
Because you weren't used to being told no.

I didn't think these thoughts would still haunt
me months later.

But now every single man I meet, in my eyes, is
a potential perpetrator.

Honeymoon

25

If it was just me and you,
Every day would be a honeymoon.
But sometimes I feel like this isn't a relationship
for two -
It's for three.
He exists in my deepest nightmares,
still stifling my screams with blood stained
white sheets,
and still tempting me to numb the pain with gin
or rum.
Forcing antidepressants down my throat,
And telling me to keep quiet.
Our honeymoon period is yet to begin,
But when it does,
I promise you
I will give you love in the purest form.